The Bulford Branch Line
and the Larkhill Military Railway

Peter A. Harding

M7 class 0-4-4T No.30041 with the branch train at Bulford Station on December 30th 1949.
John H.Meredith

Published by

Peter A. Harding

"Mossgiel", Bagshot Road, Knaphill,
Woking, Surrey GU21 2SG.
ISBN 978 0 9509414 7 9
First published 1991. Reprinted with amendments 2017.
© Peter A. Harding 1991.
Printed by Binfield Print & Design Ltd.,
Binfield Road, Byfleet Village, Surrey KT14 7PN.

Contents

Introduction	3	Timetables and Tickets	26
History of the Line	4	Closure	27
Description of the Route	11	The Present Scene	29
Motive Power and Rolling Stock	22	Conclusion	32
Operation	25	Acknowledgements	32

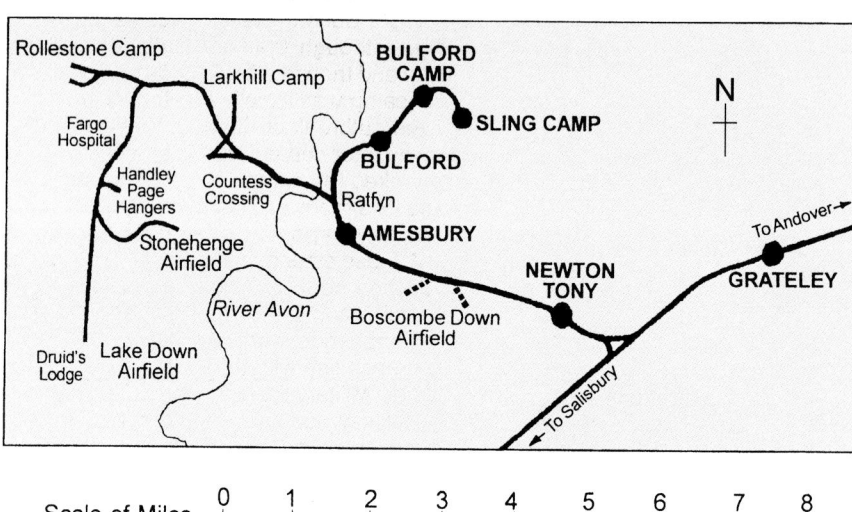

The Southern Counties Touring Society's special train 'The Hampshire Venturer' at what was normally the military only platform at Bulford Camp on March 10th 1963.　　John H.Meredith

Introduction

The branch line to Bulford was authorised under a Light Railway Order as the Amesbury & Military Camp Light Railway (Bulford Extension) in 1903 and was opened to passengers in 1906. Originally, the Amesbury & Military Camp Light Railway was authorised in 1898 to run from Grateley (on the main Waterloo-West of England line between Basingstoke and Salisbury) across the Salisbury Plain to Shrewton via Newton Tony and Amesbury. Although opened between Grateley and Amesbury in 1902, the section from Amesbury to Shrewton was never in fact built.

After the Bulford extension opened in 1906, Bulford Station became the public passenger terminus in place of Amesbury although the line continued on from Bulford for military use only to Bulford Camp and then to a final goods only terminus in an army compound at Sling Camp. This camp was initially created as an annex to Bulford Camp in 1903 and soon after the outbreak of the First World War was mainly occupied by New Zealand troops who later carved out the shape of a large Kiwi in the chalk on Beacon Hill that overlooked the camp.

With many other large military encampments already established on the Salisbury Plain, the whole line was heavily used for military purposes and, in 1914, the Larkhill Military Railway was built to connect some of these other encampments. This military railway joined the Bulford branch at a junction north of Amesbury called Ratfyn and, apart from connecting the military establishments, the Larkhill Military Railway also extended south to serve airfields at Stonehenge and Lake Down.

During the First World War, the Bulford branch line with the military extension to Bulford Camp and Sling Camp and the Larkhill Military Railway were all extensively used, and even after the Larkhill Military Railway had ceased to operate in 1928, the Bulford branch continued to serve the public and military alike especially during the Second World War.

By the 1950's, traffic had fallen away to such an extent, that it came as no great surprise when the passenger service was withdrawn in 1952 although the line remained open for goods traffic and troop trains plus the occasional 'special' train for enthusiasts until 1963 when it finally closed.

700 class 0-6-0 No.30317 leaving Bulford Station with the last out-going public passenger train on June 28th 1952. A.C.V.Kendall

History of the Line

In 1872, the sparsely populated and rather mysterious Salisbury Plain proved an ideal area for large scale military manoeuvres which were centred around Beacon Hill and a site which is now Bulford Camp. Up to this time, the Plain had hardly been a prime target for railway promotion although the City of Salisbury was already an established railway centre connecting with the London & South Western Railway (LSWR) and also the Great Western Railway (GWR).

The existing routes to Salisbury skirted the perimeter of the Plain, but a scheme devised by the LSWR to encourage some of the Bristol to London traffic away from the GWR and known as the Bristol and London & South Western Junction Railway was proposed in 1882 and a Bill was deposited before Parliament in November of that year. The planned route for this line was to branch off the main LSWR line between Basingstoke and Salisbury at about $2^1/_4$ miles west of Grateley Station and then across the Salisbury Plain by way of Amesbury and Shrewton to Westbury and then on to Bristol via either the Somerset & Dorset Joint Railway or the North Somerset Railway. Not surprisingly, the GWR were very much opposed to this scheme and the Bill was finally defeated in 1883.

Having opposed the LSWR's London to Bristol scheme, the GWR tried to push through a Bill of their own which would enable them to reach Southampton from Pewsey (on their main line between Devizes and Newbury). The route was to pass southwards from Pewsey across the Plain via the GWR station at Salisbury, and then on to Southampton through LSWR territory.

In a similar way that the GWR were able to oppose the LSWR's Bristol scheme, the LSWR were able to oppose the section from Salisbury to Southampton of the GWR's scheme, although an Act of July 16th 1883 was authorised as the Pewsey & Salisbury Railway, but this line was never built.

No further railway development was planned for the Plain until the passing of the Light Railway Act of 1896. The aim of this new Act was to provide a rather basic railway to less populated areas and farming communities by using minimum construction and operating costs without the need and expense of going before Parliament. This could be achieved with lighter permanent way, steeper gradients, sharper curves, ungated level crossings, speed restrictions and minimum signalling.

The GWR were quick to see the possibilities of this new Act and proposed a route crossing the Plain from just west of Salisbury at Bemerton to Pewsey. This scheme was very similar to their previously proposed Pewsey & Salisbury Railway of 1883. The route for this new light railway was to run up the Avon Valley from Bemerton to Amesbury via Stratford, Woodford, Durnford and Wilsford. The station at Amesbury was to be sited between Stonehenge and Amesbury with the intention of serving both places. From Amesbury the line was to run via Durrington, Netheravon, Upavon and Manningford to Pewsey. The GWR (Pewsey & Salisbury) Light Railway Order was authorised on August 6th 1898.

In the meantime, the War Department had been purchasing large areas of the Salisbury Plain and had also been negotiating with the LSWR for a light railway to run from the main LSWR Basingstoke to Salisbury line at a point just west of Grateley Station (at a similar spot to where the proposed Bristol & LSW Junction Railway had planned in 1882) and then across the Plain via Newton Tony to Amesbury and on to a terminus just east of Shrewton, making the length of the line 10 miles 62 chains. This line could then not only serve the new military camps which were being built in that area, but also the agricultural community as well. The line was authorised as the Amesbury & Military Camp Light Railway on September 28th 1898.

This latest move now meant that the Salisbury Plain had the possibility of two light railways although, without the full backing of the War Department, the GWR (Pewsey & Salisbury) Light Railway had the harder task to justify their line especially as the route was to cross about 4½ miles of War Department land. In fact, after objections from the War Department, it became impossible for the GWR to progress because their Light Railway Order of August 6th 1898 insisted that the section over the War Department land could only be built with their agreement, even though the GWR had agreed with the LSWR on August 10th 1899 that a connecting curve between both companies lines near Amesbury be built so that the section to Shrewton could be operated as a joint line.

Even at this stage, it was not just the LSWR and the GWR who had plans for a light railway over the Salisbury Plain. While all the early negotiations involving the two main companies had been going on, the local Midland & South Western Junction Railway also proposed in 1898 a scheme for a light railway from the already existing Ludgershall Station (to the east of the Plain) on their line between Andover and Savernake to run to Bulford and then on to Amesbury. Although this line never got any further than a proposal, a branch was later built from Ludgershall Station to Tidworth and was opened for military traffic in July 1901 and public passenger service on October 1st 1902.

With the backing of the War Department, the LSWR wasted no time in getting the Amesbury & Military Camp Light Railway under way and in January 1899 awarded the contract at an estimated £62,517 to J.T.Firbank who was already involved with other work in the area including constructing the Basingstoke & Alton Light Railway. Locomotives known to have been used on this new contract were Manning Wardle 0-6-0 saddle tanks "Amesbury", "Ventnor", "Ely", "Bradford" & "Amersham". Also, 0-6-0 saddle tank "Wellington" which was built by the Hunslet Engine Co. Ltd. in Leeds.

With construction well under way, the War Department either had a change of heart or were differently advised because they asked the LSWR on November 22nd 1899 if they would divert their route between Amesbury and Shrewton because, even though they had given their approval to the original route, it could still provide an obstacle while manoeuvres were taking place. The LSWR felt that it was impossible to vary their authorised route so, on November 16th 1901 they obtained an abandonment order even though J.T.Firbank had already started work just beyond Amesbury. This reduced the length of the line from the original 10 miles 62 chains to 4 miles 78 chains. To compensate Firbank, the LSWR gave him the opportunity of work elsewhere on their system.

J.T.Firbank's men laying the track (*left*) at Newton Tony and (*right*) near Amesbury. Author's Collection

Apart from the junction with the main LSWR line which was to be known as Newton Tony Junction and where a new signal box was situated, a separate single line running independently on the 'up' side of the main line between the junction and Grateley Station was also built while a new platform was added at Grateley behind the 'up' platform. This section had been authorised by an Act of August 9th 1899.

By the beginning of 1902, both the railway and the military establishments were ready for use. Strangely, although the line was authorised as a light railway, it was anything but, with heavy engineering works required to construct the line and, although originally built as a single track with steel bull headed rails weighing 87 lbs per yard, land had been obtained for double tracks which was also most unusual for a light railway.

Officially, the line was opened to goods traffic on April 26th 1902 and passengers on June 2nd 1902 but, unofficially it opened on March 21st and the *Salisbury & Winchester Journal* reported this unofficial opening in their issue of Saturday March 29th 1902 as follows:-

What might be termed an informal opening of the new railway occurred on the 21st inst. when the 3rd Battalion Lincolnshire Regiment and the 3rd Battalion East Yorkshire Regiment entrained at Amesbury Station to begin their long journey to South Africa. A large number of persons assembled to witness their departure, and as the two long trains steamed out of the station hearty cheers were given for the departing troops, which were warmly returned by the men.

When the official passenger service started on June 2nd 1902 there was no ceremonial train but, the first train to arrive at Amesbury Station did bring the morning newspapers giving news that the South African War was over. This news was certainly something to celebrate. The *Salisbury & Winchester Journal* reported this event in their issue of Saturday June 7th 1902 as follows:-

Without any formal ceremony whatever the new line from Grateley to Amesbury was opened for public use on Monday morning. A few spectators had assembled to see the first train arrive at 8.32 which brought some 15 or 16 passengers, and, what was a noticeable fact, it also brought the morning papers containing the good news that the war was over and that peace was assured. A hearty cheer was raised by those on the platform. A fair number of passengers travelled by the first 'up' train at 8.55. Some of them merely took a short trip to Newton Tony or Grateley by way of 'inaugurating' the new line.

Newton Tony Station looking towards the junction in the early years of the line. Lens of Sutton

Of the two stations on the new line, Amesbury had accommodation for loading and unloading large numbers of troops and horses plus their entire equipment as well as one military and two public passenger platforms while four long military sidings were also built on the abandoned section just beyond Amesbury Station. Newton Tony was a much smaller affair but still possessed two platforms and a passing loop as well as some sidings behind the 'up' platform.

In May 1902, the War Department requested that the line be extended from Amesbury to Bulford where a camp had already been built. A Light Railway Order was confirmed as the Amesbury & Military Camp Light Railway (Bulford Extension) on January 10th 1903.

Although the War Department had no financial interest in the original line to Amesbury, they did have an Agreement dated December 31st 1903 with the LSWR to pay $3^1/_2$% interest per annum on £28,000, representing the capital cost of the Bulford extension.

This new extension would not only serve the new camp but also the village of Bulford and was to be constructed by the LSWR's own staff (in a similar way to the construction of the Bordon Light Railway in Hampshire which opened in 1905). Work started in the early part of 1904 under the supervision of the LSWR Chief Engineer Mr. J.W. Jacomb-Hood and his assistant Mr. Short. One locomotive known to have been employed for this work was Manning Wardle 0-4-0 saddle tank No 407 (formerly called "Pioneer") which the LSWR obtained from R.T.Relf, a contractor from Oakhampton for £500 in 1881.

While all this was going on, a further development was taking place with regard to the junction with the main line. Although the Newton Tony Junction which faced Grateley was ideal for London bound traffic, it made the comparatively short journey from Amesbury and Newton Tony to Salisbury a very long winded affair indeed. With this in mind, the LSWR applied for a curve near Newton Tony Junction so that a separate junction facing Salisbury could also be built. An Order for this new junction was authorised on April 28th 1903. A direct spur of 22 chains from the main 'up' line and a 32 chain line burrowing under both main lines and connecting with the main 'down' line completed the new junction. A new signal box was also installed at the new junction which became known as Amesbury Junction and replaced the existing Newton Tony Junction box, where the original connection between the 'main' line and the branch was removed. The name Newton Tony Junction was passed on to a new small 13 lever signal box which was placed at the junction of the new curve from Salisbury and the separate single line from Grateley.

A view of Amesbury Station just after the line was opened from Grateley.　　　Author's Collection

Passenger services to Salisbury over the new curve junction commenced on August 8th 1904 and at the same time, the track between the new junction and Newton Tony Station was doubled.

The Bulford extension was completed and inspected by Major Pringle (His Majesty's Inspector of Railways) on April 3rd 1906 and found to be satisfactory to warrant his passing the line for passenger traffic. Passenger services commenced to Bulford Station on June 1st 1906 although the section to the platform at Bulford Camp was to be used for military traffic only. In fact, the line finished about $^1/_2$ mile beyond the platform at Bulford Camp in an army compound at Sling Camp which was used for goods traffic only.

With extensive manoeuvres by the Territorial Army planned in 1909, it was decided to continue the double track from Newton Tony Station to Amesbury and work was completed and ready for use on May 23th 1909. An intermediate signal box which was named Allington was also provided between Newton Tony and Amesbury stations at this time. The extension from Amesbury to Bulford was built as a single track and remained so.

An early view of Bulford Station. B.Hilton Collection

A Territorial Army regiment arriving by a special train at Amesbury Station in 1908. Author's Collection

With the outbreak of the First World War, it became apparent how important the whole Salisbury Plain area had become with many military camps already established. Some of these camps were simple tented sites and the need to turn them into more permanent establishments was now urgently required.

Sir John Jackson, the Member of Parliament for Devonport also happened to be one of the largest contractors for public building in the country and when he offered to place at Lord Kitchener's disposal any engineering assistance which he or his staff were able to give, his offer was readily accepted and he quickly got the work under way.

To help with construction, it was decided to link each camp with a railway line which could later be used as the main form of transport and the line became known as the Larkhill Military Railway. This railway was also built by Sir John Jackson who was quite an experienced railway contractor, not only in this country but also abroad. Locomotives which were used for this work were 0-4-0 saddle tank "Queen Mary" and 0-6-0 saddle tank "Westminster" (both built by Peckett & Son), 0-4-0 saddle tank "Bulford", 0-6-0T's "Salisbury" and "Yorkshire" (all built by Hudswell Clarke) and 0-6-0T "Sharpness" (built by Sharp Stewart).

Surprisingly (or maybe not so surprisingly) the line virtually followed the projected LSWR line towards Shrewton which the War Department had blocked. Commencing from a junction north of Amesbury Station known as Ratfyn on the Bulford extension, the line crossed over the River Avon by a long girder bridge and then proceeded west over the Amesbury - Netheravon Road on the level at an ungated crossing known as the Countess Crossing and then on to Larkhill Camp.

After leaving Larkhill, the line divided, one line continued on to Rollestone Camp while the other line turned in a southerly direction to Fargo where there was a hospital on the west side of the line. From here the line continued south with first a short spur turning off to the east which led to the Handley Page hangers and then a longer branch also leading off to the east to Stonehenge Airfield near the world famous Stonehenge stones. The line then continued south to Lake Down Airfield and Druid's Lodge where there was yet another camp.

The Larkhill Military Railway became one of several railways operated by the Southern Command of the Military Camp Railways. The line was worked by a railway company of the Royal Engineers who were housed in a small camp on the east side of Countess Crossing.

Like most of the military railways which were built at this time, the opening and closing dates are unclear but, it is known that on February 4th 1915 His Majesty King George V and Queen Mary accompanied by Lord Kitchener inspected the Canadian troops at Larkhill and travelled over the line in Sir John Jackson's special train. The King & Queen also reviewed the troops on the Salisbury Plain on several other occasions.

His Majesty George V and Queen Mary accompanied by Lord Kitchener leaving Larkhill on Sir John Jackson's train after inspecting the Canadian Troops on February 4th 1915. Author's Collection

0-4-0 saddle tank "Queen Mary" on the Larkhill Military Railway. Author's Collection

Although some reports state that no passengers were carried on this military railway it is understood that every Sunday in 1924 at 1300 hours a passenger carriage would be waiting at a small platform near the church at the Packway Crossing at Larkhill and anyone wishing to travel could board this carriage and arrive at Amesbury Station where the carriage would then be attached to the Salisbury train.

The first part of the Larkhill Military Railway to be closed was the section from the hospital at Fargo to the airfields at Stonehenge and Lake Down which closed in 1923.

By 1928 the complete system had ceased to operate and it is thought that by 1932 most of the track had been lifted and that by 1937 any remaining track had been removed.

The 'main' Newton Tony, Amesbury and Bulford branch was of course kept very busy leading up to and during the First World War mainly for military use, and it is interesting to note that for Christmas leave in 1914, the LSWR ran 237 'special' trains carrying about 180,000 men. Similar arrangements were made for 1915, 1916 and 1917. The arrival of the first Canadian contingent in the early part of the war, required 92 'special' trains! Later, the line passed into the hands of the Southern Railway after the 1923 grouping. The line was also very busy during the Second World War and for sometime afterwards, mainly at weekends for the benefit of troops.

By 1948 when nationalization took place and the Southern Railway became British Railway Southern Region, passenger traffic had fallen away and the line was certainly feeling the competition from the local bus service which ran a far quicker and more direct route to Salisbury.

Public passenger services were withdrawn on and from June 30th 1952 although the goods service and troop trains (as and when required) continued until March 4th 1963 plus the occasional enthusiasts special, the last one of these taking place on March 23rd 1963.

Beattie 0298 class 2-4-0WT No.30587 at the Bulford Camp platform with the Railway Enthusiasts Club special train on May 14th 1955. H.C.Casserley

Description of the Route

As previously mentioned, when first opened, the line operated from Grateley where a new platform was added and a separate line running parallel with the main 'up' line was also built but, as the local traffic was mainly interested in reaching Salisbury, the additional curve facing Salisbury was constructed in 1904 and from then on, this was the direction which most of the passenger traffic came from.

At Salisbury, trains for Bulford used Platform 6 which was at the eastern end of the station and was shared with trains for the Bournemouth line.

From Salisbury, the Bulford trains used the main 'up' line for 8 miles which included stopping at Porton and in later days Idmiston Halt (which was opened in 1943) before branching off at Amesbury Junction.

The branch to Bulford continued to curve away from the main line in a north-west direction as a double line (the other line being the branch 'up' line which joined the main 'down' line via the burrowing junction) falling at 1 in 49 as it approached the valley of the River Bourne and connected with the single line spur from Grateley at Newton Tony Junction.

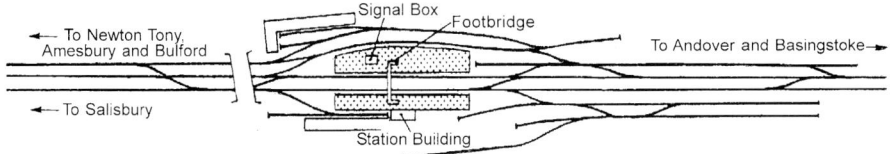

GRATELEY STATION

Grateley Station with the branch platform on the left hand side of the photograph soon after the line to Amesbury was opened.
Lens of Sutton

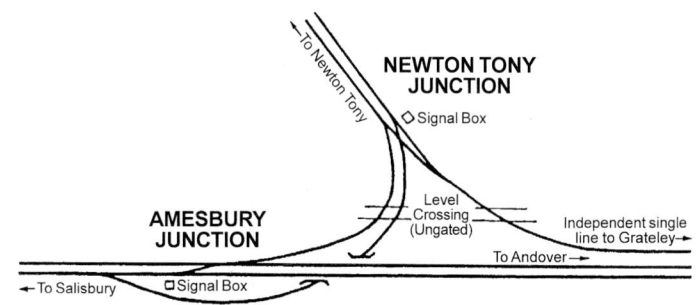

700 class 0-6-0 No.30317 and the branch train to Salisbury approaching the main line via the burrowing juction on June 26th 1952. A.C.V.Kendall

From Newton Tony Junction, the double tracked line continued for 1¼ miles passing under a road bridge and running through a cutting while falling at 1 in 100 and then climbing at 1 in 100 before reaching Newton Tony Station which was the first on the branch. The station layout consisted of a signal box and two platforms with station buildings on the 'up' platform. When the station was first opened, there were sidings behind the 'up' platform and, at a later date, a siding was added behind the 'down' platform. Just beyond the station was the only gated level crossing on the whole line. The attractive village of Newton Tony was (and still is) close by.

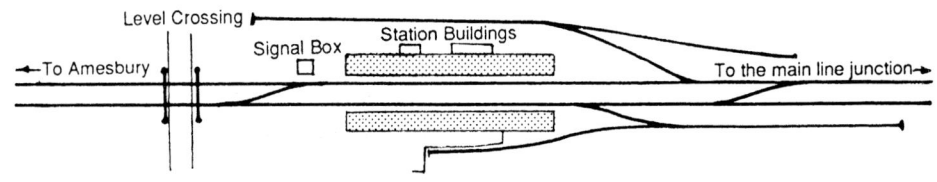

NEWTON TONY STATION

Newton Tony Station looking towards Amesbury.   Lens of Sutton

700 class 0-6-0 No.30317 approaching Newton Tony Station from the main line with the last public passenger train to Bulford on June 28th 1952.   A.C.V.Kendall

Newton Tony Station looking towards the main line junction.   J.Burrell Collection

From Newton Tony the line climbed at 1 in 55, 1 in 300 and 1 in 100 to reach the higher ground of Boscombe Down and crossed over the Salisbury - Tidworth road by bridge and passing on the left, the site of a former Air Ministry siding (in use from 1944 to 1948 to construct a large runway at Boscombe Down Airfield) and then passed on the right the site of Allington signal box which closed in 1933 before continuing on the level, mostly in a shallow cutting and then over a small country lane bridge. On the left of the line the site of the original siding into Boscombe Down Airfield was then passed where in 1917, while the main aerodrome was under construction, the siding was laid and a signal box provided but, by 1920 on completion on the work both the siding and signal box were removed.

After running through a rather deep cutting in the chalk downs and passing under first a country lane bridge and then the Porton Road bridge, the line dropped steeply to Amesbury Station which was 4³/₄ miles from the main line junction. The station here was a far cry from the typical scene of a wayside light railway station which some unsuspecting passengers might have expected. The layout consisted of two through platforms with a footbridge, signal box, turntable and numerous sidings which also included a dock for livestock, vehicles etc.

The reason for this grand layout was of course for the special military involvement which reached its peak during both world wars. When the military use slowly dropped away and the passenger service ceased in 1952, this one time impressive station became overgrown even though it was still open for goods (mainly requirements for the N.A.A.F.I.), military trains as and when required plus the occasional special train for enthusiasts. Mr. P.W.Gentry writing in the *Railway World* of August 1954 ably described the station as follows:-

The scant use made of these amenities has resulted in recent time, in the track and platforms becoming thoroughly grass grown and very woebegone, so that the onlooker might almost fancy himself in some long-lost city of a fallen empire!

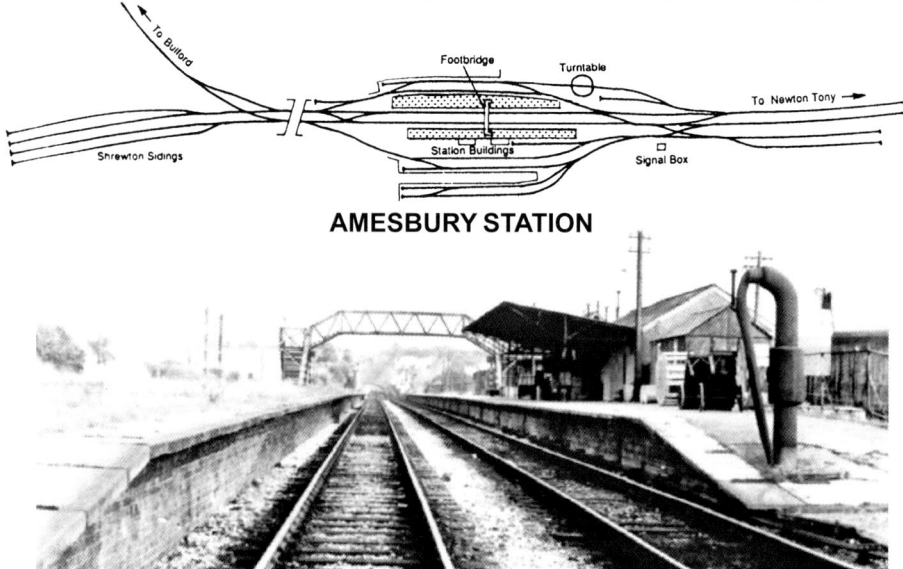

AMESBURY STATION

Amesbury Station looking towards Newton Tony.   Lens of Sutton

Amesbury Staion before the footbridge was built and showing a double shelter on the 'up' platform. This shelter was later removed and a awning was added to the station building (see photograph on the opposite page).
Lens of Sutton

Looking towards Newton Tony from the footbridge at Amesbury Station on April 28th 1928. H.C.Casserley

On leaving Amesbury Station and passing under the London Road bridge, the line passed on the left, four more military sidings which were originally built by J.T.Firbank as part of the proposed route towards Shrewton. These sidings became known as the Shrewton Sidings.

From here the line became single track only and curved north-east in the direction of Bulford, passing a short siding on the left at Ratfyn, which was from 1915 until finally closing in 1928, the junction for the Larkhill Military Railway. When this military railway opened, a signal box was provided at the junction but, by 1919, the box was closed and the junction was worked by a ground frame.

Heading towards Amesbury from Bulford on a special train which travelled the full length of the branch on May 14th 1955. H.C.Casserley

The branch continued from Ratfyn in a north-east direction climbing first a 1 in 126 and then descending at 1 in 111 before crossing over the Bulford - Amesbury road bridge, quickly followed by another bridge which crossed the Bulford - Durrington road before reaching Bulford Station. This was the terminus for the public passenger service and consisted of one concrete faced platform on the 'down' side and a run round loop. The station building was of brick and timber with a very large awning. A small signal box was also situated on the platform but was reduced to a ground frame in April 1935. The station was completed with sidings and a large goods yard.

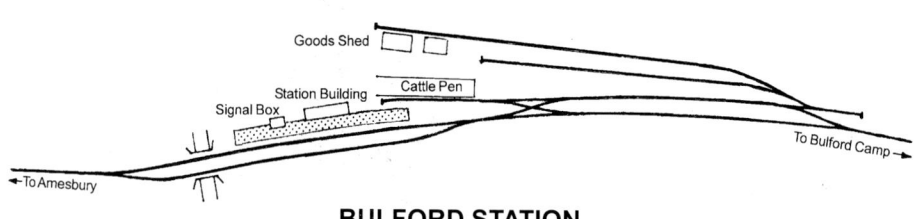

BULFORD STATION

A rare view of the entrance to Bulford Station. Norman Parker Collection

Bulford Station soon after the line was opened. This view shows the station building before the large awning was added (see photograph below). L.Campbell Collection

Bulford Station on June 23rd 1952. R.F.Roberts

From Bulford Station the line continued rising at 1 in 312 curving east and dropping at 1 in 148 and then after crossing over a road bridge, ran through a shallow cutting before climbing a 1 in 100 and reaching the platform at Bulford Camp on the level. Here the concrete faced platform was used for military purposes only and was on the 'up' side with a small booking office and a run-round loop. Extending from the run-round loop, was a long siding which ran parallel with the branch line in the direction of Bulford.

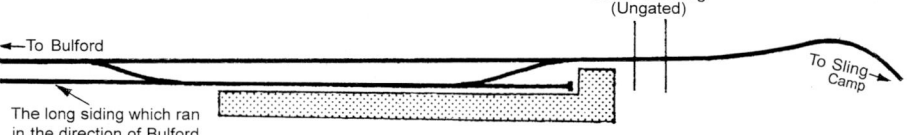

BULFORD CAMP PLATFORM

Looking towards Bulford from the platform at Bulford Camp on March 23rd 1963. R.M..Casserley

Looking towards Sling Camp from the platform at Bulford Camp on May 14th 1955. Lens of Sutton

From here, the branch continued for goods traffic only, first dropping at 1 in 100 and then climbing at 1 in 60 and 1 in 260 until it reached the final terminus in an army compound at Sling Camp (on the north side of Sling Plantation) having crossed over the Marlborough Road by an ungated level crossing. Here a platform on the 'up' side was provided with a passing loop and a siding on the south side of the platform.

In 1933 despite a proposal to extend the line over the Tidworth Road and further into Sling Camp, the short section of the Sling Camp terminus from the west side of Marlborough Road was put out of use and the track removed although the rails across Marlborough Road were left in position to preserve the right of way. In the early part of 1939 the section of line from Bulford to this revised terminus at Sling Camp was put out of use but in 1940 the line was re-opened for War Department traffic.

By 1942 the War Department requested that the Southern Railway re-open the original terminus on the east side of Marlborough Road and re-lay the track. This work was carried out by the Southern Railway's own staff and cost the War Department £450. It was also the responsibility of the War Department to provide a watchman at the level crossing over Marlborough Road as was the practice when the line was formerly in use.

In 1948 the War Department requested to the Railway Executive (Southern Region) that once again the line should be cut back to the west side of Marlborough Road.

Looking towards Sling Camp from Bulford Camp on May 14th 1955.   R.F.Roberts

SLING CAMP PLATFORM

Gradient Profile

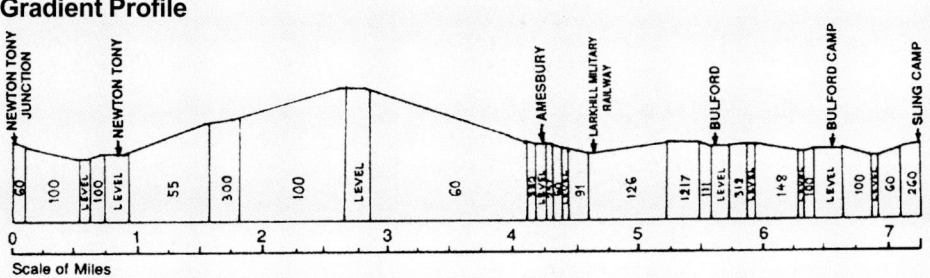

Route of the Larkhill Military Railway

The single track of the Larkhill Military Railway left the Bulford branch at Ratfyn Junction and curved to the west passing two short sidings, one leading to the Ratfyn Electricity station and the other to the military engine sheds and then crossed over the River Avon by a very long low girder bridge (some maps described this bridge as a viaduct) before the single track opened up to four tracks known as the Ratfyn Depot Sidings. From here the line became single track once more and crossed over the Amesbury-Netheravon road at an ungated level crossing known as Countess Crossing.

From Countess Crossing, the line continued towards Larkhill curving north-west and passing a siding and also one of the main features of the line, a reversing triangle which meant that a locomotive could turn to face the other way without the means of a turntable. At this point the line headed north and crossed over Fargo Road close to the junction of Lawson Road. A short distance from here, near to the western end of Colquhoun Road, a station with some sidings was situated. From this station, the line forked, the main line turning to the north-west while a branch continued north and terminated on the south side of the road which was (and still is) called the Packway.

The main line continued towards the west and then turned north-west and crossed the Packway into Larkhill Camp where, on completing a semi-circle it rejoined the Packway on the north side and then ran beside the Packway until it reached what is now Ross Road where it turned away to the north and then west to the Hamilton Battery. From here the main line turned to the south while a branch continued to Rollestone Camp where it forked, one branch leading to the camp while a short branch lead to an ammunition compound.

The main line turned to the south just beyond the Hamilton Battery and crossed over the Packway and headed towards Fargo where there was a military hospital. From here the line continued through the Fargo Plantation and across the Amesbury - Tilshead road east of the junction with the Salisbury - Shrewton road (known locally as Airmans Cross). At this point a short branch running to the east, served the

0-6-0 saddle tank "Westminster" which was one of the locomotives used on the Larkhill Military Railway poses at the end of the River Avon bridge. T.L.Fuller/Badley Collection, Royal School of Artillery, Larkhill

Handley Page aircraft hangers. The main line continued in a south-west direction before a further branch turned off to the east to serve the Stonehenge Airfield. Continuing southwards, the main line crossed what is now the A303 trunk road and ran along the east side of the Salisbury - Shrewton road until it finally terminated at the Lake Down Airfield which was at Druids Lodge.

It is interesting to note that at approximately the same spot as the reversing triangle (on the Countess Crossing to Larkhill section), a track diagram produced by G.A.Pryer and A.V.Paul in their series entitled "Track Layout Diagrams of the Southern Railway & B.R. S.R." covering Salisbury and the Test Valley shows a branch (47 chains in length) leading off to the north-east described as the "Flying Shed Branch (Balloon School)". This branch was probably laid in the very early stages of the line's construction, even before the reversing triangle and the southern section to Stonehenge and Lake Down had been completed and referred to the flying field and the Bristol Aeroplane Company hangers situated in what is now Wood Road opposite the entrance to Colquhoun Road where, in 1910, these hangers were built to accommodate the newly established Bristol Flying School and the short lived Balloon School of Larkhill.

In May 1914, the flying field closed and the Bristol Flying School moved to Brooklands in Surrey but, when war was declared in August 1914 it was not long before a large part of the flying field was used for the newly constructed hutted and tented camps, although, the hangers are still standing and are now in fact listed buildings which have been used as a storage depot in more recent times.

The "Flying Shed Branch" was built across the field for the construction of the new camps, but once the camps were completed, the branch was soon removed and no trace of this line could be seen on the Ordnance Survey map of 1926 which gave full details of this section of the Larkhill Military Railway.

A view of the Larkhill Military Railway running towards Larkhill Camp from Durrington Camp north of the Packway.   T.L.Fuller/Badley Collection, Royal School of Artillery, Larkhill

Looking north towards the Packway at Larkhill Camp, the Bristol Flying School hangers can be seen on the skyline in the top right hand corner of the photograph.   Norman Parker Collection

Motive Power and Rolling Stock

As the line was owned by the LSWR, it is not surprising that the original motive power should come from two of their most respected locomotive designers, first William Adams and then Dugald Drummond.

When the branch opened, the passenger service was mainly handled by Adams T1 and O2 class 0-4-4Ts and Jubilee class 0-4-2 engines, while the freight service was worked by his 395 class 0-6-0's. These types of locomotives were within the weight limits imposed by the Board of Trade regulations incorporated in the Light Railway Order. Because of the steep gradients, almost all troop trains and many of the freight trains had to be double headed although the Board of Trade later relaxed restrictions on certain locomotives which could be used.

In later years, Drummond M7 class 0-4-4T's and 700 class 0-6-0 tender goods were the main motive power although the occasional Bulleid Q1 class 0-6-0 was used before the line finally closed.

Troop trains used heavier engines and, after the Board of Trade relaxed the restrictions, the line was open to all classes except 4-6-0's and Merchant Navy' Pacifics. Among some of the visitors to the branch were 'Moguls' and 'Battle of Britain' 4-6-2's. These heaver engines nearly always needed pilot assistance in the shape of 4-4-0 classes T9, L11 or L12.

The branch never had an engine shed and the motive power was mainly provided by the Salisbury shed.

Standard carriage stock was nearly always used for public service, although, pull-and-push two carriage sets were sometimes used, even though the locomotives which pulled them were not motor fitted. On many occasions towards the end of passenger service, a single ex-LSWR compo brake carriage would be used with a locomotive. This practice was very much in keeping with other light railways.

M7 class 0-4-4T No.127 with the branch train at Bulford Station on July 12th 1947.   J.J.Smith

T1 class 0-4-4T No.E69 at Bulford Station on April 28th 1928. H.C.Casserley

T9 class 4-4-0 No.30719 with the branch train at Bulford Station on June 2nd 28th 1952. S.C.Nash

Q1 class 0-6-0 No.33039 at Bulford Camp platform on March 10th 1963. John H. Meredith

700 class 0-6-0 No.30317 at Bulford Station on June 23rd 1952. R.F.Roberts

The Larkhill Military Railway had its own locomotives which were housed in the two road locomotive shed at the start of the military line just west of the junction at Ratfyn. The Peckett & Son Ltd., locomotives 0-4-0 saddle tank "Queen Mary" (one report states that it was later converted to an 0-6-0) and 0-6-0 saddle tank "Westminster" were both used by Sir John Jackson in the construction of the line and camps, and were both obtained by the War Department when the work was completed. "Westminster" later moved on to the Fovant Military Railway in 1917. The Hudswell Clarke 0-6-0T "Salisbury" was delivered new to Amesbury for the Larkhill contract and like the other two mentioned locomotives was purchased by the War Department from Sir John Jackson when the line was completed. It stayed at Larkhill until 1918 when it was transferred to Longmoor.

In 1923, the Avonside built 0-6-0 saddle tank "Hampshire" was transferred to Larkhill from Longmoor, and also saw service on the Fovant Military Railway.

0-4-0 saddle tank "Queen Mary" with a group of distinguished looking gentlemen, possibly after an inspection on the Larkhill Military Railway. Author's Collection

Operation

When originally opened to Amesbury, the line was worked by the Tyer's Tablet System No.6 Instrument. The tablet sections were: (1) Newton Tony Junction to Newton Tony Station; (2) Newton Tony Station to Amesbury Station.

This later included Amesbury Station to Bulford Station when the line was extended although in 1935, the 'No Signalman Key Token' was introduced between Amesbury and Bulford.

The Board of Trade regulations incorporated in the Light Railway Order stated that no train or engine must travel over the line at a greater speed than 25 miles per hour, while, on approaching and within a distance of 300 yards of level crossings, speed must be reduced to 10 miles per hour. The Bulford extension was also subject to 10 miles per hour on curves.

700 class 0-6-0 No.30690 approaching Bulford Station with a single carriage branch train on June 19th 1952.
A.C.V.Kendall

700 class 0-6-0 No.30317 with a single carriage branch train leaving Newton Tony Station en route for Amesbury and Bulford on June 11th 1952.
A.C.V.Kendall

Timetables and Tickets

JANUARY 1944

LONDON, SALISBURY, AMESBURY, and BULFORD

Miles	Down	Week Days																				Suns		
		mrn			mrn			mrn			aft			aft			aft			aft		mrn		
	170London (W.) dep.	5L40	..	..	9R0	..	..	10 50	..	..	1250	..	..	3L30	..	..	5B35	..	..	7L35	..	11R0	..	..
—	Salisbury.......dep.	8 55	..	..	1110	..	..	1 12	..	..	3 3	..	..	5 43	..	..	7 55	..	..	9 45	..	4 30	..	..
5¾	Porton.............	9 4	..	..	1120	..	..	1 21	..	..	3 12	..	..	5 54	..	..	8 5	..	..	9 54	..	4 39	..	..
6	Idmiston Halt......	9 6	..	..	1122	..	..	1 23	..	..	3 14	..	..	5 56	..	..	8 7	..	..	9 56	..	4 41	..	..
9¼	Newton Tony.......	9 14	..	..	1130	..	..	1 31	..	..	3 22	..	..	6 4	..	..	8 15	..	..	10 4	..	4 49	..	..
12¼	Amesbury..........	9 23	..	..	1140	..	..	1 41	..	..	3 32	..	..	6 14	..	..	8 25	..	..	1014	..	4 58	..	..
14	Bulford........arr.	9 28	..	..	1145	..	..	1 46	..	..	3 37	..	..	6 19	..	..	8 30	..	..	1019	..	5 3	..	..

Miles	Up	Week Days																			Suns		
		mrn			mrn			mrn			aft			aft			aft		aft		aft		
—	Bulford........dep.	8 0	..	..	9 40	..	..	1152	..	..	1 53	..	..	3 55	..	..	6 26	..	8 38	..	5 10	..	..
1¾	Amesbury..........	8 5	..	..	9 44	..	..	1156	..	..	1 58	..	..	4 0	..	..	6 30	..	8 42	..	5 14	..	..
4½	Newton Tony.......	8 14	..	..	9 53	..	..	12 5	..	..	2 7	..	..	4 9	..	..	6 39	..	8 51	..	5 24	..	..
8	Idmiston Halt......	8 23	..	..	10 1	..	..	1213	..	..	2 15	..	..	4 17	..	..	6 47	..	8 59	..	5 32	..	..
8½	Porton 173a....[173a	8 25	..	..	10 4	..	..	1216	..	..	2 18	..	..	4 20	..	..	6 49	..	9 2	..	5 35	..	..
14	Salisbury 170, arr	8 36	..	..	10 12	..	..	1225	..	..	2 27	..	..	4 29	..	..	6 58	..	9 13	..	5 44	..	..
81½	173aLondon (W.)arr	11L9	..	..	..	..	..	2 42	..	..	5R12	..	..	6 32	..	..	10R30	..	..	..	8L27	..	..

B Via Porton. Dep 5R0 aft on Sats. via Salisbury. L Via Porton.
R Restaurant Car between Waterloo and Salisbury.

SEPTEMBER 1951

LONDON, SALISBURY, AMESBURY, and BULFORD

Miles	Down	Week Days only											
		a.m											
	50 London (W.) ....dep	11 0	..	..	..	..	..	..	..	..	..	..	..
—	Salisbury..........dep	1 0	..	..	..	..	..	..	..	..	..	..	..
5¾	Porton................	1 9	..	..	..	..	..	..	..	..	..	..	..
6	Idmiston Halt..........	1 11	..	..	..	..	..	..	..	..	..	..	..
9¼	Newton Tony...........	1 19	..	..	..	..	..	..	..	..	..	..	..
12¼	Amesbury..............	1 28	..	..	..	..	..	..	..	..	..	..	..
14	Bulford..............arr	1 33	..	..	..	..	..	..	..	..	..	..	..

Miles	Up	Week Days only										
		a.m										
—	Bulford..............dep	9 40	..	..	..	..	..	..	..	..	..	..
1¾	Amesbury..............	9 44	..	..	..	..	..	..	..	..	..	..
4½	Newton Tony...........	9 53	..	..	..	..	..	..	..	..	..	..
8	Idmiston Halt..........	10 1	..	..	..	..	..	..	..	..	..	..
8½	Porton................	10 4	..	..	..	..	..	..	..	..	..	..
14	Salisbury...........arr	10 13	..	..	..	..	..	..	..	..	..	..
[illegible]	50 London (W.).....arr	12L20	..	..	..	..	..	..	..	..	..	..

L Via Porton.

Tickets from the collections of G.R.Croughton and B.Hilton.

Closure

Having reached its peak handling the busy troop trains during both world wars, the line was beginning to feel the pinch by the late 1940's with the more local and direct bus service to Salisbury running from the centre of Amesbury. Things were not helped when the ordinary Sunday service was discontinued from May 6th 1946 because of fuel cuts, and, in 1951 the full service was temporarily suspended from February to May. When it did resume it was drastically cut to one train each way (weekdays only) leaving Bulford at 9.40 a.m. and returning from Salisbury at 1.00 p.m.

After a decision had been made to revise the 1952 Summer Timetable which would operate from Monday June 30th, a further decision was made to withdraw the passenger service completely as and from this date.

The last out-going passenger train comprising 700 class 0-6-0 No. 30317 and a single carriage left Bulford Station at 9.40 a.m. on Saturday June 28th 1952 and unlike so many other branch lines and light railways which closed at a similar time, seemed to lack the usual grand occasion with fireworks etc. Maybe the 9.40 a.m. start from Bulford did not really help! (Especially when any passengers wishing to travel on this the last train to leave Bulford, had to get to Bulford Station by their own means first!!).

This same train returned to Bulford (leaving Salisbury at 1.00 p.m. although running 10 minutes late) and was augmented with a Bulleid corridor carriage. This was the final public passenger train to arrive at Bulford Station and officially closed the service. From Bulford, this train later returned 'light' to Salisbury.

Although the passenger service was withdrawn from this date, Amesbury and Bulford Stations remained open for parcels/goods only while Newton Tony Station closed completely.

In October 1954, the double track from Newton Tony Junction to Amesbury was singled with the line through Newton Tony Station positioned so that both platforms were put out of use. The Salisbury curve at Newton Tony Junction was also taken out of use at this time.

700 class 0-6-0 No.30317 and single carriage on June 28th 1952 with the last out-going public passenger train to leave Bulford Station. A.C.V.Kendall

The line saw two daily goods trains, one from Salisbury and one from Basingstoke (both via Grateley) while a N.A.A.F.I. train ran between Amesbury and Salisbury on Mondays, Tuesdays and when required. Troop trains were also provided as and when required. The line also saw the occasional 'special' train for enthusiasts, and one advantage that these special trains achieved over the previous passenger service was to go right up the branch to the platform at Bulford Camp.

The line officially closed on March 4th 1963 although even then the Railway Enthusiasts Club special train the 'Rambling Rose' travelled over the line to Bulford Camp on March 23rd 1963 after which the track was finally lifted in July 1965.

700 class 0-6-0 No.30317 prepares to return to Salisbury running "light" with the two carriage train having closed the public passenger service on June 28th 1952. Lens of Sutton

The disused station and signal box at Newton Tony after the passenger service had been withdrawn and the double track singled so that both platforms were put out of use. Lens of Sutton

The Present Scene

The remains of the original branch platform at Grateley Station and the trackbed running parallel with the main 'up' line were both visible for many years after the branch closed but now what was the branch platform forms the edge of the station car park while the wide stretch of trackbed from here to the junction is very overgrown.

The trackbed of the former branch line (*centre of photograph*) running parallel with the main 'up' line and the remains of the original branch platform (*right*) at Grateley Station on January 22nd 1991. Author

At the junction the whole surrounding area is very overgrown, although the burrowed line which went under the main lines and linked with the main 'down' line has long been filled in.

The burrowed junction after the track was removed but before it was filled in. Lens of Sutton

From the junction, the very overgrown course of the line can easily be seen as it passes under the first overbridge on the branch and heads through a cutting towards the site of Newton Tony Station where, apart from the former stationmasters house which is now a much extended private dwelling known as Station House and some former railwaymen's cottages, there are no other visible remains to give any indication that this was ever a double track railway station although the rough outline of the trackbed can be spotted on the other side of the road where the only gated level crossing on the line was.

The trackbed from here forms a nature trail over the RSPB Winterbourne Down Nature Reserve while the abutments of the former road bridge where the line crossed over the Salisbury-Tidworth road remain and the trail continues near the Boscombe Down Airfield passing over and under disused bridges and on towards Amesbury.

The once extensive Amesbury Station has completely vanished with the building of the Solstice Park Development and the widening of the A303 truck road although the stationmasters house still remains in London Road but is now converted into flats while the former railwaymen's semi-detached cottages have been demolished.

29

At Ratfyn, the site of the former Larkhill Military Railway junction is still traceable although the former route to Bulford seems to have been completely obliterated and the bridge over the road from Bulford to Amesbury removed. At the village of Bulford, the bridge on the approach to Bulford Station which crossed over the A3028 road has also been removed and Aspire Defence now occupy the site of the former station. One interesting railway relic which reminds people of the former use of this site is an upper quadrant signal which stands at the beginning of the station approach road while some new houses which have been built near the station site are appropriately called "The Sidings".

From the site of Bulford Station a tree covered embankment gives an indication of the former route towards Bulford Camp where the long platform was visible for many years after the line closed but now seems to have completely disappeared and crumbled away under trees and vegetation. The route from here to Sling Camp can still be made out on an embankment in the middle of some woods as it curves round towards the site of the level crossing over Marlborough Road (modern maps now show this part of Marlborough Road as Sling Road).

At the Sling Camp compound it appears that following the War Department request in 1948 that the standard gauge line should once more be cut back and the buffer stops moved to the west side of Marlborough Road. Some narrow gauge tram style grooved rails (much favoured by the Admiralty) were laid down and although not used for many years are still partly visible embedded into the surface of the compound area, leading from the edge of the road to a small shed situated at the far end of the original platform (which has been filled in on both sides), the track even climbing up the slope at the nearest end of the platform. No doubt that a compromise was reached by replacing the standard gauge tracks with narrow gauge tram rails for easily moving items around the compound using smaller narrow gauge wagons.

The edge of the original Sling Camp platform with the drainage grooves still visable with the narrow gauge tram style tracks leading to the small shed at the far end of the platform on December 1st 2016.   Author

Surprisingly, it is still possible to find evidence of the Larkhill Military Railway even after so many years. The course of the line can be spotted from the junction at Ratfyn and although the low girder bridge over the River Avon has long gone, the trackbed from here to Countess Road is now a private farm track. On crossing over the road, the trackbed becomes a National Trust footpath and continues leading towards Larkhill.

The remains of the brick platform near the junction of Lawson Road and Colquhoun Road which served the stables at Strangways can still be made out even though it is much covered by undergrowth.

Little evidence of the railway remain in Larkhill Camp although the odd trace here and there can still be seen between Larkhill and Rollestone.

Very little remains of the route towards the Handley Page Hangers, Stonehenge and Lake Down Airfields and Druids Lodge to remind people that it was once possible to reach Stonehenge by train even if it was for military use only.

Some reports state that a water tower at Druids Lodge which was still standing in the 1980's was where the locomotives of the Larkhill Military Railway would take water, but, in his book *"Gunners at Larkhill"*, N.D.G.James points out that this was the water supply to the camp buildings and hangers and that the railway did not in fact reach as far as the tower.

The trackbed of the former Larkhill Military Railway looking from Countess Road towards the River Avon and the junction at Ratfyn on November 17th 2016. Author

The remains of the brick built platform which served the stables at Strangways near the junction of Lawson Road and Colquhoun Road on December 12th 2016. Author

Conclusion

There is no doubt that from the opening, the main function of the line was for military purposes although it did (in the earlier years anyway) offer local people a service which they had never experienced before. Unfortunately, even with the curved junction to Salisbury, the service was very much a 'round the houses' type of route and became easy prey for a bus service which could offer a far quicker route by road.

Not surprisingly, the passenger service was dropped in 1952 although (as mentioned) the line did manage to stay open for goods and military use until 1963.

For a light railway, the line was unique with such heavy earthworks and several other unusual features and, because of this it developed very much its own character.

Looking back through the mists of time, it is interesting to remember that the military line beyond Bulford to Bulford Camp and Sling Camp plus the complicated Larkhill Military Railway only helped to make what on first impressions might have seemed a simple country light railway into a very intriguing railway set-up indeed.

Acknowledgements

Many thanks to all the people who kindly helped by providing information and photographs for the original printing of this publication in 1991. Unfortunately, in the intervening years many have sadly passed on but, I would still like to say once more a big thank you to everyone and especially to all the photographs who kindly let me use their photographs.

For this latest printing, I would like to thank Norman Parker who kindly allowed me to use photographs from his collection and to Norman Branch for reading my text, and to James Christian of Binfield Print & Design for their help.

Since the original publication in 1991, Jeffery Grayer has brought out his highly recommended book "Rails Across The Plain" which has been published by *Noodle Books/Crecy Publishing*.

The Railway Enthusiasts Club special train the "Rambling Rose" leaving Bulford Station for Bulford Camp platform on the final trip over the line on March 23rd 1963. Norman Parker Collection